Limousine Queen

By Cynthia Kaye

DIARY OF A FEMALE CHAUFFEUR

Based On A True Story

Dedication

To all my family and friends who have supported me on this

journey. You know who you are.

I love you!

Acknowledgement

Only by the grace of God.

Partial Client List

Dr. Julius Erving NBA

Lisa Leslie NBA

Lil Wayne music artist

Anthony Allen NBA

Coy Wire sportscaster former NFL

Todd Gurley Georgia Bulldog Los Angeles Rams

Joe Theisman NFL

Newt and Callista Gingrich

The Ambassador of Quebec

Ricky Smiley comedian and host

R. Kelley video girls

Young Thug-Jeffrey Lamar Williams

Dwight Howard family NBA

Ralph Reed Fox News

Sam Champion weather anchor

Frank Brownell NRA Pres. of Brownell Firearms

Wiz Khalifa music artist

John Mayer music artist

Bishop T.D. Jakes daughter Sarah and Rev. Toure Roberts

Mike Mills of the band R.E.M.

Band members of Green Day

Government Mule drummer Peter Banta

Mary J. Blige music artist

Alicia Keys music artist

Future music artist

Birdman AKA Baby

Common actor musician

Dr. Barbara King at Fox Theatre with Tony Braxton

K. Michelle music artist

Ronald Isley of the Isley brothers

Pharrell Williams parents, Pharaoh and Carolyn Williams

Steve Harvey's pants, his assistant, father and mother-in-law

Biggie Smalls daughter, Tonya

Ayanna Fite growing up hip-hop star

Beastie Boys D.J. Hurricane's daughter

Mary J.'s stepdaughter, Brianna Latrise

Back Street Boys Brian Littrell

Snapchat President, Jeffrey Lucas

Vampire Diaries Michael Malarkey and Chris Binochu

Danita Howard, stuntwoman - Rollergirls & Captain America

Brendon Ryan Cornell - stuntman Captain America

Blake Cooper, actor The Maze Runner

ABC Executive Rebecca Campbell

Sharp Objects cast and crew

The Gospel of Kevin cast and crew

Walking Dead, Pollyanna Macintosh & Katelyn Naacon

Tom Norcliffe, Stranger Things

Wimpy Kids cast and crew

Red Band Society cast

Ricky Smiley comedian

Turner Classic Movies host and author Eddie Muller

Porsha Williams Housewives of Atlanta

Allison Janney actress

Naomi Harris actress

Octavia Spencer actress

J.K. Simmons actor of "Star" and cast

The Nice Guys with Russell Crowe and cast

Mark-Paul Gosselaar actor

Ms. Lawrence Washington Housewives of Atlanta

Godzilla crew

Scott Hall WWE Wrestler Razor Ramon Alias

Aaron Auch Silver Productions

Coran Capshaw Manager for Dave Matthews and Antebellum

Anthony Mackie Broadway actor

Derek Johnson Drama Queens

Ryan Destiny actor

Coby Bell actor

Miles Trip actor

Robert Sorcher V.P. Cartoon Network

Def Jam records executive Shawn 'Pecos' Costner

Tela the Voice

Dionne Warwick music artist

NEYO music artist

Miley Cyrus videographer Mr. Williams and daughter

Carlton Harris Ciara's father

Jeffrey Webb FIFA Soccer Commission

NBA Coach Mike Fratello

Gerald Evans CEO Hanes

Erin Collett HBO Lewis and Clark

John Ducey actor

The Voice Coach Mr. S.

Mr. McCormick Pres. Shell Oil N.E.

NFL commission Peter Abitante

Phillana Williams Arista Records

NBC President International Kevin McClellan

Troy Fluker comedian

Dave Chappelle comedian

Miles Truell actor

Leslie Boone actress

Luke James music artist

The Ambassador of Quebec

Meredith Gordo actress

Taylor Jon Smith actor

Steven Ogg Walking Dead

Pamela Nash voice on Archer

Anthony Hale actor

Alejandro Quijano actor

Baron Davis NBA

Walking Dead, Derek Fisher and Tabitha Mason

Larry Hughes NBA

Wes Robertson actor "The Thundermans"

Anna-Marie Horsford actress

As well as having the honor of driving a plethora of Bank presidents, senators, executives with Coca-Cola, KPMG, ADP, and Wall Street investment firms.

All my years behind the wheel I have managed to dodge proms, weddings, bachelor, and bachelorette trips. I have done one of each now that I see it in print I myself am amazed. And last but not least I was stood up by James Deen, Paula Deen's son, as well as Khloe Kardashian!!!!!!

Prologue

In the age of Uber and excess...By the way I was asked to be one of the first Uberettes in Atlanta and drove Travis, one of the brilliant minds behind Uber. Driving a stretch limo or even a new Caddy is not the most glamorous job. In forty years of driving, I've had some unforgettable and amazing experiences. Most of what I've seen and experienced has changed my views of the rich and famous and even your average Joe.

More than half of my life I have been driving and serving the rich and famous from high-powered executives and their mistresses to rock stars and Hollywood A-listers. Starting from the first day on the job with a fresh face and the energy of the 18-year-old that I was, I always kept a notebook by my side. At first, I used the notebook to write down the names and addresses that dispatch sent me. But after my first few "encounters" with strange sorts I started to use it as a journal. After all the years of chronicling the crazy the amazing and the excess baggage of the people that I had the pleasure (and I use that term loosely) of chauffeuring around.

I knew the day would come when I was ready to share my stories because they are just too unbelievable, incredible and juicy to keep to myself. So here it is, life in Mama's Limo. Get ready to take a ride in the fleet of Mama's cars and experience the reality of the privileged, over-sexed legends and genuinely good people.... I won't deny you these stories as well. Join me for a fast ride through the city filled with scandal wannabes, and others with shocking stories.

Forty years of notebooks documenting crazy people, their crazy stories, and some downright crazy nights. You never know what will happen when the limo doors close and the engine purrs. Sex, drugs, and rock-n-roll is just the beginning. I couldn't make up these stories if I tried. You would think that since I'm the driver and because I have the passenger's lives in my hand that this 100-pound lady would be given respect. However, once you immerse yourself into my stories, you will see that that's not always the case.

P.S. Coolest night off - chauffeured in an 18 passenger stretch in mint condition Concert at Charlotte Coliseum the band Kansas and none other than Van Halen! Years later Limo, Van Halen in Atlanta!

I am telling my trips as a chauffeur in no order, I am going with whatever and that is my prerogative!!!

Chapter 1: How It All Began

I have procrastinated until I have lost my filter. I promised myself not to put my stories on print for readers until my mother was long gone out of respect for her but the truth being told she knew me deeper than anyone and carried a many of my episodes to the hereafter with her, WHAT A COMRADE SHE WAS TO ME, I LOVE YOU MOTHER! E. E. Cummings quote: "I carry your heart (I carry it in my heart)".

I have always loved cars. My first episode was when I was 12 years old and I decided to play hooky from church (a big part of my roots) and joyride in one of my dad's cars Sunday afternoon. I waited for my parents to go to church and I called my girlfriend to join me for a trip to the ballpark where all the boys were. On the way to the ballpark we stopped by McDonalds to grab a milkshake and french fries. At the park the four on the floor got stuck in the mud, and the cutest boy in the park was so impressed with my driving skills, he asked me to the school dance and became my first boyfriend. When we arrived back at my house, we placed the car in the exact spot we took it from so my parents would not notice it had been moved. We were so pleased with ourselves until my dad came in holding a french fry asking "What you were thinking?" He did not mention or notice the mud filled tread on the tires. As I grew older my passion for driving grew as well. Girlfriends and family long before I was licensed, and back in the day it was easy to get away with not so much today, were all driven crazy with my wanting to be behind the wheel and they let me. I simply wore them down with my persistence and they taught me a lot. As I got older limousines came into play from proms as well as evenings of culture and concerts topped with weddings and girls' night out. I took notice of how much the chauffeur was making and decided to be at the party as well as get paid.

Since I was a young girl, I had my eyes on the nicest cars on the lot. I was 18 and didn't see any Royce's in the near future but I had a brilliant idea. I would find people in town who owned my dream cars but could not drive them for whatever reasons. I could be their personal driver. And what better place to advertise my ingenuous new business than the richest town in the city: Buckhead. The calls and requests came flooding in. Of course, when you a young woman dealing with rich guys with amazing cars, you are bound to encounter all sorts of nuts and perverts. And boy did I. I am sharing my stories in no specific order, putting pen to paper as I like! They are my stories and I am sticking to them! I may be a bit detailed if you have a weak stomach you might want to drink milk!

As a personal driver one of my first encounters was the son of a boxer in Vegas, he lived in a high-rise in Buckhead, he was handsome and wealthy. He owned an Excalibur classic car, with a long body, two seats, sitting low to the road, and wonderful curves, it was quite the eye catcher! We had a bite to eat at one of my favorite establishments, R. Thomas (by the way it is an amazing story in itself, it has exotic birds, wonderful greenery, healthy menu, they lost the key so they decided to remain open 24/7 ,365 days a year.

Now comes the unexpected, he suggests I come up to his place for my check, which I reply I will wait downstairs, he is all of the sudden quite demanding, I agreed and within a few minutes he became "Dr. Jekyll / Mr. Hyde". As we entered his apartment the phone rings, as if we are being watched it was his ex-girlfriend, after he hangs up he begins to sob and tell me of the heartache she caused and how he hung her over the balcony by her ankles. He lived on the third floor, I exited stage left as quick as possible! I learned a life lesson you nor I can put a price on, your good looks may get you in the door but your brain and kindness will keep you there as well as give you the sense to know when to leave!

My next client owned a chain of hair salons on the east coast. He was a functioning alcoholic with a fabulous Rolls Royce. He enjoyed going out to the dance clubs, but did not want to risk a DUI, that is where I came in. He appeared to be classy, as we learned in the previous story, and to quote my beautiful mother, "Believe half of what you see and nothing you hear"! With that in mind I am tuned into my space always having to be on guard has kept me from harm more than once.

Sad to say I have learned it is not people I do not trust it is the evil inside! I also learned money does not buy class, by the end of the long club hopping night, he wanted to pay me for my driving services with sex. Needless to say Mama got her money. I put him in a taxi and drove the Rolls to his office, there was a bottle of Moet in the backseat which I gifted to myself and left the keys in its place! My next client was a manager for a famous rock band, he was from Atlanta, he had heard about me from mutual friends, contacted me to drive him and a friend in his Bentley for the evening.

The usual scene club to club, as the sun was rising, I told him we needed gas, he slurred "Bentleys do not run out of gas" as I pulled into the hotel lot sure enough we ran out of gas. I ask the door man to take me to get a tank of gas upon our return my clients had forgotten that I was driving. One of them got behind the wheel intoxicated cranked the car put it in drive and went straight into the ditch grill first. The local police had already been summoned as well as a wrecker. I asked the officer if I could get my shoes out of the trunk. I got my shoes and lucky enough without any questions I got out of there.

For security reasons I needed more structure so I decided to get my chauffeur license to work for a limousine company. Before I give you a glimpse into my world behind the wheel, I am going to break down the main "industry terms" we drivers use on the job.

Dispatch: I have had the fortune of working for some of the biggest car services in the business. They have a fleet of cars at the client's request available for me. From Escalades, Cadillac sedans, and Suburbans to Lincoln Town Cars and stretch limos, they have it all. And, on a rare occasion, they have even offered a Rolls Royce or two.

My favorite car to drive, hands down, is the new Cadillac. Back in the day, I just loved the 18 passengers stretch Lincoln limo. Nothing compares to that baby.

But before I gush and dish out all the dirty secrets and crazy stars that have been in my car I am going to give you a quick look inside at the workings of our business. As with any profession we have a process that begins with the client requests and ends with the client drop off by me.

Dispatch arranges the time and date of the pick-up and destination as well as the type of vehicle. When it's my turn, they call me and I promptly respond with a confirmation. From that point on, it's up to me to impress the client. As a rule, I am always 15 minutes early. I make sure to allow the time for traffic and any pop-up incidents.

The Greeters: Most entertainer's and famous clients have what we call greeters. The greeter and I coordinate the information that I have received from dispatch. For example, when the plane pulls up to the gate, they call me and give me the heads up. I pull up at that point and await the approach of the client and their luggage. Once the client and their belongings are safe and happy, the greeter and I say our good-byes and I take over.

The Pickup: After introductions I ask the client when opening the door for them, is there anything you need before we arrive at your destination. The response is usually "no one has ever asked me that." The key to being a good limo driver is always trying to anticipate what the client might need and to provide them with the best service. I offer them water, give them the chance to choose the radio station and make sure the car is a good temperature for them. If all goes without a hitch, I then proceed on the road and to their destination.

The Drop Off: When the client exits, I call dispatch and inform them that the ride is complete and the mission accomplished. Usually, dispatch will respond with "good job" or some other type of pat on the back and we begin to discuss the details about my next trip.

Chapter 2: Birdman And Bugatti – Rapper's Delight

My motto has always been "Hurry up and wait! But tonight, that motto takes on a whole new meaning. Thirty minutes pass and I barely start to fidget. I am used to this. Another thirty minutes. And then another. Finally, my cell phone vibrates and I answer before the ringer goes off.

"Hello," I say.

"Pull around to the red Bugatti and we will be with you shortly," Birdman's assistant Greg tells me.

"Yeah right! This ain't my first rodeo," I want to yell back. "I could go run a mile and be back behind this wheel without you noticing."

But of course, I don't.

"Yes, sir," I reply.

And I wait. And wait. An hour passes before I spot the entourage, the client and his assistant exit outside. His assistant gets in the front passenger seat. I smiled and kept my eyes on the Red Bugatti to my right. Out of nowhere two men, strapped with high power guns jump in the back seat. The third row was a guy who Greg referred to as the mechanic.

"Is there something I should know," I asked in shock. "Do I need to throw on my bullet proof vest and helmet?", I then asked half-jokingly. "And while you are at it pull your pants up".

"Baby is wearing $6 million in diamonds," Greg says as I twitch. Before I continue, it's probably smart that I tell you who my client du jour is and what the fuss is about. Birdman, aka Baby, is a rapper as well as the CEO of Cash Money Records. And according to my latest Google search, he is known for throwing his jewels and money around.

And our convoy begins — the Bugatti, my limo, the tour bus and many friends in their private cars. The Bugatti pulls out and enters the highway at approximately 90 mph maneuvering through the city. As we all follow, the "mechanic" starts screaming at me to hurry up (his first mistake was screaming at me while I was driving). At this point I am in full concentration mode, although traffic is light, nutty drivers keep trying to get in between the Bugatti and myself. I ignore the screams from the back seat and keep driving and following bumper to bumper, when my speedometer hit 100 mph, I was done.

"He can kill himself but he is not taking me with him," I said slowing down to a much more comfortable speed on the highway. "What are you doing?" comes the voice from the back. "Keep up or he will get lost."

"If he doesn't know where he is going then he should be following us," I snap back.

Tonight, was a birthday celebration for friend and fellow rapper, Young Thug. I am relieved for a moment as we pull up to the destination and park off to the side near the Bugatti. Before I can even relax, everyone is back in their cars and we are off.

At the next spot, I prepare myself for a longer wait. When the tour bus driver invited me to come aboard and watch a movie, I was all too happy to indulge. But that did not last long. Five minutes later, Birdman and Young Thug come onto the bus and tell us to leave. Confused but professional, I quickly hopped off. Before I even got back to my car, I notice the blinds on the bus shut and I see it rocking back and forth. Wow didn't expect that.

The next stop of the evening is a seedy club on Old National Highway. I had no address, but was instructed to follow Birdman.

"Stay on their tail, or there will be hell to pay.", comes the voice from the back. "I am doing this cat. You hold on to the tail", I cut back to him hoping my venom will shut this guy's trap. No such luck.

But I have to admit when I realized the part of town this next club was in, I was happy to have the armed men in my corner (or at least my backseat). We arrive safely, thanks to me, and the tour bus parks and the Bugatti is backed up against the wall. People were getting loud and belligerent I thought as I took the post in between the guards. With one standing on each side of me, I felt so secure. All of the sudden this little punk from out of nowhere tries to challenge them saying he is part of this gang and he demands to be noticed and allowed entrance through the back door. Normally I would have exited stage left to avoid confrontation but surrounded by AKs and lots of muscle gave me quite the sense of security. False or over confident. Either way for a brief moment I was invincible.

After a short time thank goodness, the gang exited the club and we are off. This time for a video shoot. His assistant jumps in car and we go to the bank to pick up 5k for an outfit for Birdman. We deliver money to a fashion coordinator at Saks Fifth Avenue. They stay on the bus, so it's just me and the assistant in the limo. We are following the bus to Fulton Industrial Boulevard to a warehouse where they have these fab Rolls Royce's they are going to use in this shoot. Lots of people are there, it's about 8pm. They did not start shooting until 1am. It started to pour down rain and they asked me to go to Walmart with the fashion coordinator to get some leggings. Now its 2am at this point, and the Walmart is miles away. On my way back as I pulled off the exit, I notice that it is blocked. A couple of police officers standing by the police ribbon, I inquired to them as to what is going on

They told me that guys were shooting each other. One is dead and they are blocking the exit ramp. I explained what I was doing. Pleading with them they finally let me through. When I get back to the warehouse with supplies at six in the morning they let me go. The next night, Birdman's assistant calls and requests my services for the evening. They will be shooting another video. Still tired from the previous day I rally and head over to their Midtown hotel. It was a birthday celebration for Young Thug who was in the Bugatti with Birdman. Next stop a gas station. What a crew: my limo, the Bugatti, a fabulous Rolls and classics in mint condition. The assistant and I remained in the limo as everyone went into the store and I asked "Which one is Babyface?" He replied he was the one with the tattoos on his face going down his neck. Okay, back to admiring the cars. The chap owns the Rolls whom I had ironically spoken with on the phone just hours earlier about driving for him. Everyone had grabbed their mixers and snacks and reentered the limo, and we are off to the next club. Thank goodness I keep a small cooler with my goodies. Why you ask? Because I am left outside all by my lonesome. I break open my cooler as they enter the recording studio, and I am assuming it is going to be a really long night.

As I am standing outside of the studio when two of my colleagues drive up in limos. Someone to talk to help pass the time. Babyface, Young Thug and their large crew exit the studio and park the Bugatti across the street and set up bright lights and the videographer takes their place in front of the car and begins to record.

As I'm watching I'm thinking "that's all you've got as far as dancing goes...let this little lady show you how to move".

Hours later they are still filming and the sun is coming up. I was asked to take Youngblood to his car. My partner and the mechanic got into an awful brawl. My partner thought it was too dangerous for me to take Youngblood by myself he insisted that he do it. I fought back knowing that I could go home after.

I was exhausted. We are looking at 14 hours now. That's a long day to be with this entourage as Youngblood got in my limo. "I am scared of you", I thought to myself. I guess maybe I should have listened to my partner. I was just so anxious to get home, but I always keep pepper spray in my reach. I took him to his destination at the art complex. Strange night, strange morning and stranger humans.

P.S. I learned the definition of MAKING IT RAIN: Birdman tosses hundreds of dollars in a crowd! You will not see me diving for it. How about MAKING IT RAIN in the Limo?! No, luck as well as no tip!!!!

Chapter 3: Ambassador To Quebec

This client is classy, he and his staff are visiting Atlanta for multiple meetings which I have no idea the subject matter nor am I supposed to know. I am on call for all staff members to take them where and when they desire. Dining, shopping, etc. I have the privilege, as well, of driving the ambassador's wife. She is a pretty, quiet, classy lady. It was a long week of hurry up and wait part of the job sitting outside wonderful dining establishments mansions and hotels. I myself venture in as well out of view and remain at a minute notice for the client. You never know what may occur. I often picture myself in a role reversal. The time has come to drive them to the Air Force base. I am the lead driver with the ambassador and his wife with multiple motorcycle police in front, on the side as well as a fleet of limos following my lead and two motorcycle police riding behind.

As we enter the Air Force base we are led to the tarmac. We are to pull up to the quite large aircraft passenger door of the limo lined up to the plane door. I exit the limo and open the door for the wife first, southern charm you know, with the assistance of our fab service men. Protocol being order of the chauffeurs in line to bid to formally say our good-byes, and I may as well say anticipating a FAT TIP, as the ambassador followed by his entourage shook each chauffeur's hand I noticed he would hand them a token of some sort. As he reached me he kissed me on both cheeks and placed his home land flag on my lapel. As he is conversing with me, one of the motorcycle police had been attempting in a Neanderthal manner to talk to me and rolls his front tire on my heel. I remained composed while internally dealing with excruciating pain.

As they boarded the aircraft we all extended what I know as a homecoming wave. We are not to enter limos until the craft is in flight. This gives Neanderthal the green light to taunt me. His goal it seemed was to test my professional manner. I am assuming it was a lack of attention in his childhood. After what seemed like an eternity with him underfoot it is time to leave in the same manner we arrived, dignified. A long week at work, long hours in the formal service industry and again no monetary gratuity. I still have the pin and the memory. And every now and then I can now laugh at the bold but hardheaded policeman.

Chapter 4: Dr. Julius Erving

I have the great pleasure tonight of driving the one and only Dr. J. As I wait for him to come up the escalator from the terminal I am star struck which does not happen to me often, as I am used to driving people in the limelight. When I see him turn the corner to meet me he is being bombarded by fans and I am overwhelmed how he greets each fan taking the time to sign autographs as well as agree to photos with the fans. I see a lot of entertainers I have driven do everything they can to avoid their fans, which in my opinion without your fans, you are really not a star. I knew off the bat, he was a different breed with his approachable demeanor.

As we are walking to the limo fans are still stopping him and he graciously obliges each and every one of them for an autograph. He is walking so fast my petite legs can hardly keep up so I express to him he needs to slow down or carry me. We both laugh and he graciously waits for me to catch up. I open the door and comment as to what a tall drink of water he is. I get in the

driver's seat and ask if there are any stops he would like to make
.He replies, "No thank you."

As I enter the highway he asked how traffic is. I tell him it is clear sailing but as fate would have it there was an incident to cause a delay. As we are sitting, he strikes up a conversation asking me about myself, if I have children, etc. I returned the question, and he said several with his youngest being eight. I commented "Can you say condom?" and we both laughed. He said his youngest keeps him young!

Traffic began to move as we spoke about the crazy growth Atlanta was going through and how the roads were getting there but not quite ready. I told him I had been here all my life and could remember when the population was six hundred thousand and Atlanta could not wait until it was one million. Now it is six million. As we arrived at the destination he was such a gentleman. He expressed how much he enjoyed our conversation and tipped me graciously.

Chapter 5: Lisa Leslie

Today I am driving a female basketball superstar, Lisa Leslie.

What an athlete this woman is. I am totally honored to be in her

presence as I have a superstar athlete daughter myself and I

know first-hand what dedication, drive, discipline, as well as

determination it takes having seen it in my daughter. Lisa is a

looker as well and has a pleasant personality. We did not

converse much but as she exited the limo she offered me her

bottled water and white cheddar popcorn. In all my years that

was a first!

Chapter 6: Porsha Williams Housewives Of Atlanta

This evening I am driving Porsha Williams. It is about eleven at night and she has sunglasses on, I comment jokingly that there were no paparazzi around and she could relax. I don't think she found any humor in my comment. I am driving her to my assigned destination that she requested. I drive her to a different address. As, I pulled up to the Nikko Bistro, she asked me to pull around back to the garage and wait until her companion arrived. As we waited she chatted a bit about current events, as a handsome gentleman approaches the limo she asked me not to drive off before they departed. He opened the door and she handed me one hundred dollars folded neatly as she exited the car and bid me a goodnight. I thought to myself I will sit here for as long as you like if you keep handing me HUNS!

Chapter 7: Housewives And Hair

Today is a beautiful day and I am excited to meet a particular client who I have heard a lot about in the local and even national news. His name is Lawrence Washington and from what I understand he is the best of the best among hairdressers. He is the official hairdresser of the Housewives Of Atlanta and now he has his very own show. Well, today I have the pleasure of picking him up from his salon. I am excited because I have never driven Mr. Washington, I mean Ms. Washington. According to dispatch, he likes to be addressed as a Ms. The ride went well and I just loved Ms. Lawrence. What a hoot.

After driving him or her a couple more times, all formalities were out of the way and I referred to him as Girlie-girl! He is just too cute! And he struts in heels better than I ever thought of doing and I do it well. I cannot help but overhear his conversation as he is sucking on ribs and talking with someone whom is obviously more than a friend as I am hearing bits and pieces of sexual content per their chat. It is starting to disturb me, as well as distract me. About that time, he asked me to pull over in a less than desirable part of town to dispose of the rib bones. I suggest we wait for a safer and more suitable spot as he replies, "girl I was raised in the hood, I am not afraid." As I pull over he is still talking the talk, tosses the bones and we are off to the airport. I pull up curbside, open the passenger door, and offer him a wet wipe for his hands. As I gather his luggage, I am thinking a wet wipe would have been in order for his conversation as well. He is reaching in his pocket and says as he has previously, "Oh girl I will catch you later on the tip." Whatever, I thought, and bid good-bye on to the next trip. GIDDY-UP!!!

Chapter 8: The Voice Coach - Mr. S.

On to the truly talented and beautiful people. This client, I call him Mr. S, is a voice coach to some of the most talented humans whom voices I would trade my pinky nail (just the tip) to have: Madonna, Justin Timberlake, Christina Aguilera, Jennifer Hudson, wow! He's a personable, intelligent man. I have driven him before, the first time my limo lot pass was malfunctioning, so I asked the limo lot attendant if it would be okay for me to park on the side. Sunday afternoon, slow day in the limo lot, she says okay. When I come out with Mr. S., she has the transportation police and is writing me a ticket. I tell the officer this attendant here gave me permission; the attendant replies I never spoke to this lady. "Oh, my", I'm thinking then I blurt out to the attendant while you are throwing me under the bus are you going to kiss me? I took the ticket, drove my understanding classy client home. By the way, it was thrown out of court. Justice ruled.

Chapter 9: Dionne Warwick - A Legend In San Jose

Do you know the way to San Jose? I have listened to this legend all of my life. What an exciting evening. It began, however, in one of my not so favorite vehicles: a van. I was dispatched to a fabulous local hotel to pick up a band. Not thinking about it as I approached the hotel, one of my colleagues was departing in a Lincoln Town Car. The band was standing out front with instruments. I gathered them all comfortably, strapped them in, and away we went to the venue, one I had never been to on the outside of town. Good-looking group of talented "cats". They were all doing their own thing: talking on the phone, texting, emails, etc. When we arrived at the venue, pulled into the garage, they exited the van along with the instruments and asked me to please return at 11pm. The time now is 7pm. One of the band members blurted and added that you are more than welcome to wait backstage and enjoy the show. I was so excited to see the show. Wow. I am backstage at a Dionne Warwick concert. Have I died and gone to "San Jose?" I am thrilled to be here. The acoustics were impeccable. The sound was music to my ears and she looked incredible. After the show the boys loaded the van, and Dionne changed into a cute warm-up suit. I must say she has maintained her appearance and her gifted voice. She puts the absolute D in Diva. Assuming as I never should, we were headed back to the hotel Ms. Dionne decided to take all of us out to a late dinner. A place I had never heard of called "This is It BBQ". And boy is that an understatement. The food was wonderful and the company even better. After everyone had acquired a full belly, we returned to the hotel and they generously tipped and we said our good-byes. What a great night with a legend.

Chapter 10: Wiz Khalifa

Tonight is the birthday bash and I am so excited. The night begins with a fleet of limos at the talent entrance to this particularly large venue. You name them in the hip-hop industry and they are here. I am driving the entourage for a guy by the name of Wiz Khalifa. I had never even heard of him before this evening. I kept asking "What is a wiz?" Apparently from what I am being told, he is the new "Bob Marley". Rumor has it that he is very smart. I don't get it but the crowd seems to love him.

Wiz exits the venue and naturally, young people are all around the limos for a look-see at the talent and I am very impressed with the way his security team handles the crowd. They put Wiz in the limo in front of me with security guards and the rest jumped in my car. His assistant rode with me. Cool dude, his name is Nate, very sweet and personable. Naturally I blurt "pull your pants up" to no avail. We all went to a local hip-hop club called The Compound. I had never heard of it but it was slammed with music artists, locals and visitors for the birthday bash. I was falling in love with all of the fantastic cars. I believe every policeman was on duty in the city for this event.

As my clients exit the limo they request I pick them up at the back of the club at 3am. It is now midnight. I parked at the local diner one block from the club. Best to be close to client drop-off in case of an early departure. A co-worker and I decide to grab a bite at Waffle House while we wait. As soon as we sat down, the booth next to us was assaulted by a quite larger than life younger woman wearing a halter which was not covering much and cut off jeans that showed her butt cheeks with red kiss lip tattoos, and let's not forget the stilettos.

As she attempted to enter the normal sized booth, she had to lift her belly fat over the table and slide in. About that time we received a call from our clients to pick them up. No worries I exclaimed to the waitress as I slap down a few dollars and run to the car. The crowd was incredible and obnoxious. The back door (as requested) was so congested and as I am driving the crowd is trying to see who is in my limo. I grab my guts and cruised slowly through this crowd. Thankfully the police are guiding me to my destination. The fans are knocking on the windows yelling and screaming "who is in there?" Needless to say it was a little unnerving.

All of the sudden a young woman bumps the front of the limo and exclaims "she tried to hit me". The officer next to my driver's window says to me, "No worries ma'am, I saw everything. I've got this." and gently escorts her off into the distance. She is still screaming "she tried to hit me, take her to jail", I thought to myself if I am going to jail it is because I did hit her! After 30 minutes, which by the way seemed like hours, my clients exited the club. The paparazzi were everywhere and the fans were delighted by the willingness of the artists to allow them photos and autographs. To my dismay I am blocked and cornered and have to forward and reverse with no assistance. (Which by the way I am completely competent. Did I mention I can drive anything from a 3 on the tree to an 18 passenger stretch?) With the intoxicated crowd I am being careful and trust me they are no help.

All of the sudden my clients are entering and exiting the limo and the artist who I will refer to has the name of the popular stick of gum (Juicy) and a few straggling with the crowd good looking women, Wiz – some guy in a Rolls who I am blocking decided to join us. His name is Jay-Z. This is not going to end any time soon. But I can spot Jay-Z a mile away and it's pretty cool that this hip-hop legend is in my back seat. Still stuck, I notice the Rolls in front of me trying to make its exit. They honk. I am usually on top of everyone exiting and entering the limo but it was so hectic I did not notice Jay-Z exit my car.

"There is nowhere to go, dude!" I yell, getting more anxious by the minute. Before I hit full blown panic mode, Jay-Z appears from the backseat of the Rolls and sends a whistle to the crowd. Like magic the crowd backed up and no less than ten police escorts come to attention and guide me to the road to safety. Wow I think. Jay-Z must have a magic whistle.

Either way lesson learned. Do not get yourself blocked in anywhere ever again. I drop my clients off at the hotel where they are to catch a nap and back off again. Wow, I am exhausted, I don't know how they do it. Oh yes, I know they love what they do.

Firing up blunts. I am the lead car in the fleet. I leave everybody because I will not get pulled over. I am just as guilty at this point. They are drinking and smoking and they are not to do that if it does not have a partition. Got them back to the hotel, no tip and no thank you.

Following weekend Wiz is back in town. They call me and want to do a night of clubs. I started out driving the manager on errands: food, adult novelty, drugstore etc. We arrive at a friend's home. I am stuck sitting in the limo several hours, my body gets restless. Finally, the many men enter the car and off we go. We went to strip club first. On the way some of the guys were talking about how they had devirginized the girls at the last party. It made me uncomfortable, which I knew that is exactly what they had in mind. They did not get a reaction from me, although it is hard to shut passengers out with no partition. The majority of hip-hop artists request an SUV. As I entered the club lot I pulled to the door. I can maneuver any car in a crowd, traffic, etc. I watched these young people with money and high dollar driving machines, jewels, excuse me BLING-BLING, into the joint one after the next. The usually quite large club security men search everyone and everything. It actually is CRAZY. Almost every trip is more extreme than the last.

I can't imagine the constant partying and little privacy. There's a price you pay in the spotlight. I sat for hours, stunned. Time goes by and I know it is my career and I make the best of it with a positive manner. My clients come out and want to go across the street to this club called Mansion. Five minutes after they went in my phone vibrated. "Will you bring our weed inside?" the caller mumbled. "We left it in the limo."

"No sir," I said with confidence. I am surrounded by officers.

The place is slammed. There are at least 500 people outside waiting and they are up to capacity. All of these people can't be hip-hoppers or dope dealers. If not, I wonder where does all this money come from? Maybe I am in the wrong profession. As Wiz and his entourage exit the club he is asked by many fans for a photo opportunity. He never hesitates through the night to oblige the many requests from his fans. I am impressed that he has not forgotten how he became famous. He enters my limo and his assistant tells him he is in the wrong limo and he says, "Oh no, I am not, Mama is driving me home." When we arrive at the hotel his entourage is quite buzzed. I might add, they leave him to me to take care of, so naturally I do.

As I open his passenger door he is asleep, better than saying passed out. I say to him "Wiz wake up." as he slowly looks up at me he says "Oh thank you Mama for always getting me home." I had to laugh as I tell him you are not home honey, you are in Atlanta at the hotel. He grabbed what was left of his quite large bottle of rum and exited my car as the sun rose over the city. I drove off thinking all that adult babysitting and again NO TIP! At least he said, thank you. And not to mention they left blunts all in the limo, it took days and a lot of detail to get it right for future clients!

Chapter 11: Music Madness

I get a call to pick up Shawn Costner at St. Regis, Buckhead. It is Music Midtown as well as BET awards weekend. According to my sheet, he is a bigwig, executive at Def Jam Records. He has a lady whom I presumed to be. I stopped presuming a long time ago as I have learned not to guess. They ask to go to STK in Midtown for dinner. She gets out of the car. He asks me to go "pick up the third of their threesome." Alrighty then I think. I am to pick her up at the lower south terminal at the airport. Not one to judge, I say okay and head to the airport to grab this mysterious third party. She gets in the car and starts talking to me in a Jersey accent that is better than birth control. Not being told differently, I proceed to STK.

"No," she says when I inform her of the destination. "Please take me to the hotel. I need to freshen up."

She promised to be ready to go in 10-15 minutes, but I did not hold my breath. Sure enough, 90 minutes she slides into the backseat transformed into a vixen and sporting a nice buzz. We go to STK and by this time Music Midtown, a local concert, is buzzing. Streets are slammed. I could get her within a block to the restaurant. I told them to call and I would pick up in the same spot. The three got in the car along with owner of Magic City, the notorious strip club in Atlanta. Magic, as I call him, is laying it on thick flirting and grinning. I continue to drive and proceed to Prive, a Midtown nightspot where Future is hosting a birthday bash for Shawn. While I am parked on the curb next to the club I am standing next to an officer when the police dispatch a call over the speaker on his shoulder that a silver Dodge Charger driving south on Spring Street and the corner of 14th Street was shooting a weapon randomly up. I put myself apparently a little too close to the back of the officer as he says to me "Lady what are you doing"? I reply,"You are the closest one in a bulletproof vest!"

About that time, dispatch says he has been apprehended and my nerves are shot. Thank goodness that is all. I turn around to see now what all the fuss is about and there is a man exiting a Bentley and he begins to urinate on the tire. The crowd starts exiting the club and most of the females are carrying their stilettos as well as their eyelashes. I had to laugh. Two completely intoxicated ladies, barely recognizable from the ones I drove earlier in the night, hop in the back seat followed by their man, Shawn Costner.

"It's his birthday," they cooed. "Do you want to help us sing Happy Birthday?"

I politely smiled, eyes on the road but managed to sing a one liner of Happy Birthday, Mr. President. I had a feeling that "singing Happy Birthday" entailed a little more than a song. I was right. The oohing and ahhing began and as I looked in the rear-view mirror, quickly averting my eyes when I saw what was going on. I heard moaning and groaning, as the duo proceeded to blow out the birthday candle. I adjusted my inside rear-view to look at the ceiling. Even I am not old enough to see what was going on in the backseat. Our car can't go any faster. I am tempted to close my eyes, but I can't do that while I am driving. Instead, I used my two side view mirrors for the rest of the ride and just for laughs made a sharp turn to the destination. My clients were sliding across the backseat but managed to keep a grip on the cocktails. As they all rolled out of the limo they thanked me with blurred verbiage and tipped me generously. Oh, what a night.

Chapter 12: Coming Out In The City

The BET awards is still in town and I am picking up a single passenger. He is an attractive 30ish guy and he tells me he is a hip-hop DJ in Chicago. He also announces in one breath that he has come out to his radio audience that he is gay. Oh well. A new one for me. I couldn't care less of his sexual preferences. As a matter of fact, I have a lot of gay clients and friends. He exits the limo and I advise him of the pickup location.

Later that evening. There was a private undisclosed location (I am assuming a local hip-hopper home), pajama party he was excited to be attending. Sounds like fun I said. We parted ways and I wonder to this day why people feel relaxed enough in my presence in the back of the limo for true confession, cleaning of the mind and soul. No worries, I am cool enough to take it with a grain of salt and drive on. Giddy up.

This is a big weekend in Atlanta. It is Music Midtown and the BET Awards. Naturally, every good voice is in town for one reason or another. I am to pick up John Mayer and his band and take them to their hotel, the W Midtown. The BET awards is also the same weekend. I meet the band at FBO where private jets come in behind Hartsfield. I never did figure out which one of the guys was John Mayer. They all had on hats and were quiet. They were friendly and tipped me a crisp Benjamin. Later I got a call to pick up Khloe Kardashian. I was so excited that I even went and got a trim and manicure just for her. But it ended up being one big let down. Early as usual, and anxiously awaiting my VIP client, I got a call from her greeter telling me that she had decided to ride with her friend and my services were not needed. I am so livid. Was this a setup, I wonder to myself? I can see her and I can see the greeter from a distance. But being the professional that I am I answer the next call. This one is to pick up the band Green Day and take them to the airport. I do just that. Thrill ticket. Then I get a call from a strange number, with a Los Angeles area code. I am thinking is it Khloe trying to reach me. The caller is whispering and asking me to pick her up at the W Midtown which is coincidentally where I happened to be. I explain I am picking up another client and cannot offer assistance. The NBA finals are in town I am thinking that must be what Khloe stood me up for!

Chapter 13: I'm Not Gonna Cry

Mary J. Blige has come to town. She is doing a radio show and I pick up her and her assistant and her bodyguard out of a Porsche SUV at the lower south terminal. I am to go to St. Regis but stop per request. First I was to go to Busy Bees soul food restaurant. Upon arrival the bodyguard sitting in the front-seat tells me notto pull into the parking lot so we are not blocked. As we enter the restaurant, Mary J. wants a private dining area. The manager says they don't have one and she'll have to sit in the only dining room like everyone else. Keep in mind this place is crowded and there are people waiting in line to be seated. She turns to her assistant and says, "You know what I want so I am going to go back to hotel."

I drop them off at the St. Regis and go back to get the assistant. 4 huge bags fried chicken, 4 veggies, smothered chicken and pie. I thought what an appetite Mary J. has.

The next Mary J. trip is for a documentary she is doing. When I pick her up I asked if there were any stops she would like to make before the hotel. She says no and I say "What no Busy Bees?" She says "No thank you I am on a diet." and I blurt "Well you can have half a pie." Whoops!!!! I drop them off later at the theater. The next day I pick them up and take them to the private air base. I love going there because I get to pull directly on the tarmac to the jet, meet the pilots, and go in and get treats. I am happy with my service rendered to my client and often wonder if they are or even consider me as a human being. Maybe I put too much thought into taking care of them and in reality, I am offended when I am not shown the same respect. I do have their lives in my hands behind the wheel and they will show gratitude to a door man before me. Blows my mind.

Chapter 14: The Grizzly

The interesting charters keep coming! This evening, I am dispatched to pick up a single woman and take her to the local sports arena. She tips generously as she exits the limo and tells me she will call me 15 minutes prior to the end of the game. It is bitter cold and the police won't let anyone park on the curb. After circling 10 to 12 times she exits the venue. "I am a popsicle" she shivers. I was to return her to the hotel when she directs me to the players entrance and out comes a 6'4" man whom enters the limo and announces he is hungry and wants to dine at one of the local hotels.

Normally I am sure whatever Anthony "Tony" Allen wants he gets. I tell him the kitchens are probably closed and I suggest my favorite late-night seafood place. He agrees that will be fine and as coincidence would have it he had dined there before when he was in town. She did not care for the old house and blurts in a high voice that she would not eat there and he tells her to wait in the limo. I found it amusing as it is one of my A list go-to establishments. As he exited, she followed. Several employees of the restaurant came out and asked me if I could get autographs for them of this NBA player. I regretfully had to say no but advised them to reach out themselves. I find most are apt to oblige to their fans. As they re-entered the limo, he directed me to a local strip club. It is one that I myself consider seedy, but what do I know? The time now is midnight and it is 12 degrees and I bundle up and run the heat for seven-minute intervals (company rules) and watch as young thirty-somethings clad in Gucci flood the scene. I stare in awe as these young people throw money around the outside of the club. I can only imagine the cash flow on the inside.

Wow, I thought, don't these guys and gals have jobs and go to school? It was a Wednesday night and they were rolling. And I wanted to crawl under my plush remote-control electric blanket. They exit the club blitzed, not the comfy couple they entered the club as. Upon entering the limo he is on his cell and she says "that better be your wife and not some other bitch." He pulls his cell phone back to raise his hand to her. About that time we are pulling into the hotel. She jumps out of the car and he ends the call almost in tears. He says to me "I miss my wife I want to go home."

I said I think that is a wonderful idea as he gathers his composure, which I am sure he needs all the pro-baller strength he can muster after telling me they drank a bottle of tequila in the strip club. He exits the limo tossing fifty dollar bills in the front seat. I like it like that!

Chapter 15: Razor Ramon Scott Oliver

They call him Razor Ramon. Scott Oliver Hall is his birth name and he is a now semi-retired World Championship Wrestler. I arrived at the pick up to find no one answering the door. I did not have a direct contact number and I called dispatch which advised me to wait. Shortly thereafter a very tall attractive stumbling man exited a car and approached mine and advised me he would be there shortly. As usual, shortly means much longer than Webster's definition. No matter, I am on the ticking clock. As he exits the home, he seemed to have grown a foot without changing his heel height. I did not recognize him, mainly because I do not watch wrestling. Not my idea of sport. I am just saying!

As he enters the limo I proceed to greet him and ask if there are any stops he would like to make. He suggests I climb in the back and we make out. He is pretty cute, I am thinking. I could definitely do worse. As he exits the limo, I find out who he is. The producer of whatever show greets us and apologizes for anything he may have said and I returned with "I am a big girl and can handle the big guy". They were doing a documentary about his wrestling career as he was being inducted into the Hall of Fame for the WWF World Wrestling Federation and/or WCW World Championship Wrestling. He called me the next week and asked me to join him at the induction. Nice guy, really cute too. Afterwards I Googled him. He has had his share of being the drama king but to me he seems to be a little more grounded and realizes what is important...family and doing the next right thing.

Chapter 16: Hands Off Kid!

Well this next guy could use a few tips on being grounded and doing the next right thing. This trip starts with what I presume to be a normal pick up at the airport and drop off at a residence but much to my dismay my young 20ish client with the look of innocence turned into a rascal. Rascal you say? Let me begin. Cruising along the highway at an appropriate speed on a Friday, traffic volume high, this young lad, a mere child to me is telling me all about his girlfriend, college studies, etc. I am driving in the far-left lane next to the median wall. He is sharing with me his plans for a family member's wedding in Las Vegas and everyone was meeting at his aunt's house her in town to fly together for the nuptials.

He exits his seat belt and he sits behind me and tells me I look tense and could use a shoulder rub. In shock, I tell him he needs to get back in his seat belt, but he continues to rub my shoulders. Feeling agitated I demand he return to his seat belt, all of the sudden he reaches in my blouse and teases my breast and attempts to bite my neck. When I blurt out "get your testosterone raging butt back in your seat before you make me wreck you little twit!!! He does return to his seat blushing and quiet as he can be, utters here is a $20 tip for you. I do not know if my aunt will come out and tip you and I replied "I am not going to have the time to meet your aunt you, need to prepare to roll out as soon as we reach your destination. " As we approached his residence I inquired as to what made him act in the manner he did. He said it was a fantasy and I replied, "It's a good thing I am not a male chauffeur!

Chapter 17: Ne-Yo

I may not know the hottest rappers without a quick Google search, but I am definitely up to par on Ne-Yo's hit records. Full disclosure: his real name, TK, did not ring any bells but the dispatch gave me a heads up before I headed out for the pickup.

The first few times I drove Ne-Yo were some of the most boring and uneventful rides of my life. He was like a robot and he never even smiled or said thanks. I mean, I get that he is a big star, but after the third or fourth time taking him to the airport or taking him home from the airport, you would think he would say something. I mean, really?

Maybe it was the extra coffee I had slung back during lunch or maybe I just hit the breaking point with the silent treatment. I picked him up on a beautiful summer evening. He, as per usual, left his luggage and hopped in the back seat where he proceeded to put on his headphones and stare out the window. The whole ride to his mansion, I kept looking back trying to meet his eye. The lack of contact was frustrating and I was sick of it.

I pulled up his driveway and hopped out grabbing his luggage out the trunk before he even had time to unbuckle his seat belt and get out of the car. I must be quick because his bags were at the front door and I was back at the car as soon as he was closing the door. Backpack and headphones on, Ne-Yo had his eyes to the ground. Then out of nowhere he comes up to the car door. I exit to speak with him and he picks me up and twirls me around, WOW REALLY!? I was speechless only to respond by saying "was that my tip?" He smiled and walked in the house.

As I drove away I started to fume for some reason other than the fact I was missing Cinco De Mayo with my friends. I was in a hurry to catch up with them when I see blue lights in the rear-view. I pull over to a safe place and the officer asked me if I knew why he pulled me over. I reply "I hope it is not because you are lonely". I giggled he did not. I explained my actions and he told me to slow down. Making a living on the road you are bound to get the BLUES every now and then!

Not too long after I was assigned the not so pleasure of picking up Ne-Yo's fiancée, Crystal Renay Williams. She was rude off the bat as well as too big for her britches so to speak with a bad attitude not only with me. Her snubbing was overdone to any service individual. I remained a lady and was directed way out of the way to pick up the house key. I was not happy that I was not going to the wonderful posh gated community I usually drive Ne-Yo's family as well. Instead I am an errand girl on unlit back roads on what seemed to be an unusually unorganized venture. She gets out of the car grabs the key and remarks upon her return how much she loved her future mother-in-law. I could not believe my ears, she is human. Now we are off to find a house in the middle of nowhere and when we arrived I almost fell out of the car. I could not believe my eyes. The house was nothing compared to the wonderful residence Ne-Yo is accustomed to. Oh well, not my business. No surprise, there was

no thank you and no tip.

Chapter 18: Ciara's Dad

So, a few days later I get a call to pick up Ciara's dad. He has requested he come off the road in his present position and accompany her overseas to an exotic destination. I don't know if it is for work or pleasure but I myself would love to go there. He is to take care of the new baby. I love babies. He is really handsome man and is telling me how disappointed he is about his daughter's relationship with Future. How he had been caught cheating on Ciara and how unbelievable that is because she is such a beautiful woman inside and out. She told her father - only to quote him "Daddy he didn't mean it, he won't do it again. Wrong baby girl, he does not deserve you and he will do it again, once a cheat, always a cheat." Kind of ironic because "Daddy" was telling me he had put a PI on his wife and Ciara's mom because he thought she was cheating.

Oh, what a tangled web we weave. I am so embarrassed to say that if he ever caught her cheating he would like me to join him for dinner - which I declined. I thought to myself the Troglodyte does not fall far from the Neanderthal.

Chapter 19: Kristy Lee Cook

Oh, what a breath of fresh air, I am picking up the cutest freshest young artist I have seen in a long time named Kristy Lee Cook. She and her mom are a delight. Her mom and I engaged in a mature female conversation to the airport. I think we may have even made cute Kristy blush as they exited the limo. I tell you, Kristy has not yet learned how to pack light. Although in her defense she was at the recording studio late nights all weekend and photo shoots so I am sure they had to bring a bit of everything. I commented on her guitar case. She said that it along with the guitar were a gift from an accomplished musician whom swore her to secrecy. I admired that statement at her young age and that she reached in her own wallet to tip me instead of looking to mom to do it. Lots of luck girlie girl, you are on the right track. Miss Kristy Lee Cook with a guitar in one hand and a Gucci hat box in the other. Kristy Lee was up in the air for her future and up in the air back home for a break.

Chapter 20: Newt Gingrich

To the zoo you say, I love the zoo. Knowing I am not going to go in I am like a child still excited thinking about all of the wonderful animals and exotic birds. My trip says Gingrich but I am so rushed and busy I don't think it is Newt, especially going to the zoo. Okay, so I was wrong once but even then, I was mistaken. LOL. I greet my former political client's present wife and grandchildren. We are dropping the grandkids off which I find really bizarre, we are going to the zoo you know? Anyway, minding my own business I am told where they live. As Newt is trying to direct me, I exclaim I got this, this is my town. I was raised and grew up here (stomping ground you know). Within a five-mile radius.

As I look back at him in the rear-view mirror he appears to be a little disgruntled with me so I pull my charm card and schmooze his mood. As the kids exit the limo they all say their good-byes and Calista requests entrance to the back to enter their luggage for a tie change. She says to me "does this match?" and with my fantastic sense of fashion I had to say no ma'am it clashes with your jacket. She replies, "see I told you." Newt grunted and rolled his eyes and of course changed his tie.

At once we all reentered the limo, buckled up, and headed out. Ironically the Susan G. Komen Walk For The Cure was in progress. The attendees are so cute, I love pink and they are adorned in pink tutus like ballerinas. Ironically, my client had asked his wife for a divorce after having a double mastectomy for breast cancer to marry his current wife according to Google. (I love Googling) Shame on him and her. I could not resist putting it out there how wonderful these walkers were, showing so much compassion for the men and women who were struck with breast cancer. Some may call it tactless, I call it on and to the point.

After the zoo, I dropped them at the airport. Needless to say no tip and he acted like he could not get out quick enough. Calista was pleasant and said she had to make a hair appointment which I found strange because her hair was perfect and had not moved all day. Oh well, happy flying to you and your family.

Later I was asked by my boyfriend if they tipped me generously and my reply was NO TIP to him in a text, I accidentally sent it to Calista, WHOOPS! She replied, I am sorry we thought everything was taken care of. I thought to myself, oh my how am I going to fix this? I sent her a reply, stating I sent it to the wrong person and that it was my pleasure. Read your text before you hit send in the future.

Chapter 21: Dr. Frisky

Today I am in a stretch-limo to pick up a doctor to take him to the airport. When I arrive, he is scattered and not quite ready and asks me to help. Oh goody I thought just what I don't want to do. It helped that he was handsome so I gave him assistance so we could depart quicker, time is money in my business. As we head to the airport he lowers the partition and leans over my shoulder, never a good sign as well as he breaks my eyes from the road.

He starts with unwanted sexual conversation and all of the sudden comes through the partition and tries to forcefully check my tonsil. Little does he know I had them removed at a young age. I am so aggravated by his actions trying to remain calm and drive at the same time. I politely ask him to return to his seat. He does not listen, so I raise the partition and pull the fuse out of the overhead. This is not my first rodeo. We pull into the airport and he is acting like a scolded child. I had to smile. As I am gathering his luggage he tips me a hundred, guilt and shame money I guess. I bid him a safe trip and he has the nerve to ask

me if he can call. I simply reply no thank you and say good-bye.

Another trip, another nut!

Chapter 22: Ronald Isley

I am thrilled, today I am picking up a legend for an evening with the stars at the Civic Center. His name is Ronald Isley of the Isley brothers. As he exits the hotel I am beside myself with blood rushing through my veins. This is not normal for me. I pride myself with not being starstruck but not today. I introduce myself as the family enters the car. As we are in route to the event I notice the young child is not in a seat- belt and request that Mr. Isley would be so kind as to put his grandson in a secure seat. He replies, "that is my son." Oh, my, I am thinking, can you say condom? He has got to at least be in his late seventies by now. Wow, more power to him, I hope GOD has given him a strong heart. His beautiful much younger wife attends to the child almost upon arrival to the event.

They all exit the limo and Mr. Biggs and I coordinate their pick-up. Upon their return to the limo I ask if they are going to attend the after party which he replies "No thank you." About that time dispatch calls me and requests that I do not drive by the homeless shelter/soup kitchen for there is always a lot of commotion on the outside. Mr. Biggs asked me what the conversation was about and I tell him. He replies "You go the way you normally would go, I have seen my share of shelters and street people." So off we drive, by the shelter and Mr. Biggs says "look at that man pissing on the man in the sleeping bag" and his lovely, yet most likely sheltered lifestyle wife responds "oh my goodness I cannot believe he is urinating on that man and why are they all standing around Gladys Knight Chicken And Waffles?" And Mr. Biggs and I both had to laugh and I respond "the homeless like to smell chicken too." I enjoyed that before, some reason it brought an icon down to earth for me. What a great guy. We said our good-byes and I was giving Mr. Biggs his hotel umbrella and he told me to keep it. I still have it and will not let anyone use my Mr. Bigg's umbrella!

Chapter 23: Future

Today, I am dispatched out of church per request by a client for a white female. I asked them if the client was bold enough to say that out loud and they said yes. His name is Future, and I have no idea who he is so naturally I Google him. Oh Lord, my past has finally caught up with my Future! As the greeter brings him to the lower curbside pickup, I am standing at the Escalade passenger door. By the way, most hip-hop artists request an Escalade. I do not know why, they are sitting on a truck frame and ride rough. As he enters the limo I asked him to pull up his pants before he talked to me. He looked at me like I had lost my mind and told me to wait a minute, he was waiting on a package.

"A package?", I respond "What kind of package? I don't do packages." About that time the rear passenger door opens behind me and sure enough there is the mystery package. Oh well so much for listening to me. I drive off and he is talking to a woman I am gathering by his responses when he says to her "you know how to swim?" I found that to be strange. I was on the swim team and assumed everyone knew how to swim. Any how the conversation started to get a little too sexual for my comfort zone, so I tuned him out. Naturally that was the same time he started asking me if I knew where he was going. I respond, that of course I do and like most male clients they still have to try to direct poor little me. My strong self always replies, "I've got this cat, you just try to hold on to the tail." As we arrive at the destination it is Ciara's high-rise. He is still trying to tell me how to pull up to the door and then he says, "Oh I see you have been here before." He literally jumps out of the car holding his pants with one hand and his mystery package with the other. No thank you and no tip!

Chapter 24: Common

There is nothing common about this guy. As he and his assistant come up the escalator, fans are coming out of nowhere to ask for his autograph. Not having time to Google him before the pickup I ask "should I know you?" and he replies "I am an actor on a series Hell On Wheels." I have not seen it I reply but I will be sure to. He says he is a music artist as well. We arrive in the limo lot and as I open the door he says "allow me please ma'am." Wow, I am taken back by that and he requests that I go ahead and start the car. He and his assistant Melissa are chatting about his itinerary, quite a heavy schedule, when he says to me "Please take us to the Atlanta Fish Market." Naturally, I comply.

As they return to the limo after dinner he is smitten with a woman whom is exiting the restaurant and hangs out the window as the limo is in motion expressing his fondness so to speak. We arrive at the hotel a few blocks away and I tell them I will see them in the morning for their departure. Melissa hands a twenty-dollar bill to me and tells me thank you.

The next day Upon arrival Melissa tells me, Common will be down in a few and she is going across the street for coffee. I offer to give her a ride but she thought it better I wait in case he comes down before her return. I agree and about the time she walks off he appears. He bids me a good morning, enters the limo and ask If I would like to hear his new song? I reply, "of course, I would. "So, he sings to me the whole way to the airport. Hugs me upon exiting and Melissa tips me another twenty.

Chapter 25: Alicia Keys

What an amazing artist. The trip begins as usual when I arrive. I let the contact I have know that I am there. At this point I have no idea whom I am driving. The voice on the other end tells me they will be out shortly which almost never happens and today is no different. I have been to this residence many times before. It is the parents of Swizz Beatz.

The first time I drove his parents his mother got upset with me because what she thought was the long way was my way of avoiding traffic for us. I do know what I am doing behind the wheel. I did my best to remain professional, she sure tested me. I did not expect a tip after that and I did not receive one. Much to my dismay she exited the garage door and came to my window and tells me "my daughter-in-law is from Los-Angeles and you only need to say hello to her." I think, "Wow, really?" as I roll up the window hoping she will get that I do not appreciate her belittling tone.

Time is going by very slow now and after what seems like eternity I see a small man exit the front door with luggage. He is pleasant and introduces himself as the assistant. Assistant, to whom I still don't know, says he will be back shortly. Another hour goes by and he returns with more luggage, as I am helping him, a little boy comes up to me and ask me my name. I reply "Cynthia and yours?" He says my name is Egypt but everybody calls me EG and you can call me EG too. What a doll. Then EG says I like your Escalade, I have a Ferrari. Oh my, how cute is he I thought. About that time, I am putting two and two together and realize it is Alicia Keys. Oh my, one of my favorite artists of all times. We all get settled for a long trip to a friend's house that is way, way out in the country. She is so down to earth and appears to be a great mom. She is feeding EG grapes and they are talking and laughing. It was a delight to be a part of it. As we arrive at the destination, I was a little disappointed. No thank you, no good-bye, no tip. I can't believe it sometimes but I have to remember it is a long fall off the pedestal I put some of these

limelight people on!

Chapter 26: Joe Theisman - Break A Leg

I am thrilled today to meet not only a football legend but one of the most handsome men on the planet. Joe is in Atlanta for a Revco Beauty convention at the World Congress Center. I am his handler to get him from one venue to the other. The company has me in the back of the stretch with an assigned driver for the entire weekend. I arrive at the Westin on Friday morning and when I see him for the first time in person, I am like a schoolgirl with a mad crush. I brought my daughter with me and was to put her in a taxi to follow. Joe insisted she ride with us and we were pleased, what a guy. Years later, when her Papa Len passed, we found out he knew Joe quite well. He was the voice of the Washington Redskins. Small, small world. First, on the itinerary was an interview with a local television station, then a question and answer period for fans, along with an autograph signing of footballs then we took a lunch break. Joe could have opted to dine without me but he chose to have me accompany him. Next, we met all of the other stars.

Ahmad Rashad, Billy Dee Williams, Danny Glover, Vendela and soap opera actors from various shows. Now it is time for dinner and my daughter and I went home conversing about the great day we both had. The next morning, I greet Joe for another day of events. Afterward Joe decided to partake in a few libations which was relaxing for him and he wanted to drive the stretch limo which we had to decline his request. I still thought he was the hottest man I had ever seen. Next day I enter the Westin to meet Joe, it is the last day and his wife has come into town to join him. She is a pretty woman and the first thing she says to me is "Do you have a lint brush and baby oil?" Really? I sent her to the front desk. After shaking my head a few times to get over her abruptness, we all headed to the limo and over to the convention center for the last day. Had a great weekend, just being that close to a legend in my favorite sport. Every now and then I Google him to see if he is still as handsome. He never disappoints!!!

Chapter 27: Bachelor Gone Crazy

Tonight, I am doing a favor for a friend with a couple of stretch limos, not a large company. My pick-up is at 8pm. It is a bachelor party. Naturally the first thing I am told is to head to the Cheetah a gentleman's club in Midtown Atlanta. As we approach the club the bachelor says to me "We have decided to drive all around town instead of going in." They direct me to Buckhead and it is slammed with cars and people walking everywhere. The guys have the sunroof open and they are having a blast howling at all the women. At one point they are helping women through the sunroof into the limo. This is unnerving for me. They do not care and it is getting late and I remind them their time is up. They did not want to extend their time, so I proceeded to the destination. When we arrived, I asked them to settle the bill with me and they suggest I strip for the fee as they opted not to go to the strip clubs. What the hell are you taking about?! I got so mad I could not see straight. They told me to come inside and they would pay me. I never dreamed they would start manhandling me and trying to tear my clothes. It was scary and I ran out of the house in fear, jumped in the car and screeched off. Needless to say, they were successful in not paying me but the next day they had to deal with the owners of the limo face to face. Never again will I work for an independent. They do not get a credit card upfront. It is too risky and as well as bachelor parties. What a joke. I pity the bride of this groom. WHAT A PIG! On my way home, my nerves were shot and I noticed a car with its emergency flashers on and shortly after a woman walking on the side of the road. The car appeared to be fairly new and it was about 2am. I know how scary it can be so I pulled over to assist her and she ran into the grass of the yield. I exited the car and yelled "Hello, I am a woman by myself, I only want to help!" She flagged me the no thanks gesture and started running. I yelled again, "It is not safe, let me help you!" She finally gave in and as she approached the car I rolled down all of the windows and turned on the inside lights so she could see that I truly was alone. She opted to get in the back and I asked her where she would like me to take her. She said the next exit, her boyfriend was coming to get her. As we pull up to the gas station she asked me what she owed me and I replied nothing, it is what we should do for each other. The next morning, I found a twenty-dollar bill in my purse, she had slipped in. Cool!

Chapter 28: Van Halen

Tonight, I am a client in a stretch limo to the Van Halen and Kansas concert at the Charlotte Coliseum. The music is out of this world and afterwards I am backstage with the band. I am leaned against the wall when the door opens next to me and Eddie Van Halen pulls out on his motorcycle. As he turns his front wheel barely tips the toe of my cowboy boot. My girlfriend shrills, "Are you okay, he ran over your toe?" "Of course, I am okay, that was Eddie Van Halen!" Oh, my goodness, Eddie Van Halen ran over my toe. I could not have been giddier! Needless to say, I still get a thrill to this day when I think about it. Years later in Atlanta my girlfriend has tickets to Van Halen. I cannot make his concert but I am able to attend the after party at the hotel with the band. My friend and I are sitting at the bar when Eddie Van Halen walks up next to me. I introduce myself and my friend tells him of the motorcycle-boot episode. He begins to tell me how sorry he is about that and lifts my foot up and kisses it. I almost fell off the bar stool. Thank goodness I had a pedicure that very day. My friend takes a picture and his

bodyguard grabs the camera and pulls the film out. That tells

you how long ago that was. FILM!!!!! Anyway, I couldn't have

cared less, I had the experience no one could take away. Eddie

was escorted to his room and the band asked us if we would like

to come up to the party. It was a grand room with a baby grand

piano. As we begin to mingle this one particular woman

followed me all around the room. When she began rubbing my

arm telling me what beautiful skin I had, it was time to go. Still

all and all I had a great night out not behind the wheel!

Chapter 29: Evening With The Stars

Tonight, I have the pleasure of escorting the parents of the fabulous Pharrell Lanscilo Williams, Pharoah and Carolyn. Two of the kindest, sweetest, attractive, graceful---stop me now I could go on and on. Mr. Pharoah, personality plus. A short distance to the venue, I bid them a pleasant fun-time. I would have pleasure, much pleasure in attending such an event. The talent was the best of the best. As I reenter my limo, I see in the distance, a white vanned out truck, the metallic paint gave that away. Not too much gets by me as a petite female in a predominately mancave world of chauffeurs, I am quite unique. It does not hurt as well that I have a lot of street sense. That being said, I peek around the corner to see who exits, Its Usher. oh yes, what a voice. As he exited, I gasped with the moment. It was too cool. He entered the backstage where I had the honor of enjoying the buffet. It was quite different for me having spent time at hip-hop studios where no one ever thinks about offering so much as a chicken wing. Tonight, I am having crab cake. One of my favorite edibles. It is time to stage the limo for my clients'

exit. I am always on top of their needs and convenience, it is

who I am, it is what I do. I want to do as I would have done unto

me, old school so to speak and I have had success thus far with

that work ethic. As I stand by the main exit, straight ahead so

there is no niche upon exiting the event, the style in which they

entered, the Williams' immediately eye to eye contact enter the

car smiling from ear to ear. We converse of the great artist and

are mingling as we pull into the hotel. They both hug me and sir

tipped me graciously, class to the top of the glass.

Chapter 30: Anna-Marie Horsford

Next day, I have the pleasure of escorting Anna-Marie Horsford to a Midtown live stage performance. My only option for her hurried time frame was to pull on the left of a one way to the curb and have her slide to proper safety. Most always I pull up with the passenger door for the celebrity and the handlers behind me and bodyguards in the front beside me. Lord knows I would not want anything to happen to that sweet soul nor any of my clients. I feel responsible, no matter gender, muscles or age. She placed a gratuity on my shoulder and told me not to get out, naturally I exit the limo and she rushed to her play. You go my lady nice to meet you. I drove her to airport early the next day to depart Atlanta. I walked her luggage all the way to the desk, she tipped me and hugged me good-bye and expressed her satisfaction with me personally, as well my service. My pleasure.

Chapter 31: R.E.M.

Athens band, first pick up Mike Mills son Julian, in black car service. We do a multitude of genres, I love it and the families are a part of the package. I may drive them for years without meeting the star of the family, not that they all are not stars in their own right. Julian is coming into Atlanta on a holiday from college. Cool name, Julian and laid back vibe. He conversed with me and we had what I call a pleasant, not a lot of empty air, two-hour trip. I dropped him at the destination, shortly he returns with a monetary tip. Thank you, I respond and tell him it was all my pleasure. Not too much longer, I am picking up Mike's friend, she is as down to earth as Julian we had a great conversation. On another trip I pick up his long-time friend, his wife, and daughter for a trip to the Braves baseball game. Pick up in Athens, drive to Atlanta for the game and back to Athens to drop off, great tip and then I cruise back to Atlanta. Wow! Almost three years later, I finally get a trip to pick up the multi-talented artist I had been wanting to meet. I can tell when clients do not want to converse and he hardly spoke. I could not hear a sound cold deaf. Oh well. Dropped him and my thousand questions I had for him. Sometimes silence is golden. Nice to finally meet you Mike Mills.

Chapter 32: Bulldog Country

Today, I am picking up the amazing Bulldog team member Todd Gurley at the Atlanta airport and driving him to Athens. He puts his headphones on and looks down at his phone, the hour and a half drive, chewing gum to the beat. I looked in the rear-view mirror, one too many times and had to abruptly apply my brakes at which point he catches my eye in the rear-view as he looks to see why I had done such. I think it startled us both and I kept my eyes on the road. It is not like me to stare. We arrive at his destination and he exits the limo, headphones and phone. No thank you and no good-bye. I still have the package of gum he left in the limo. Good luck in your pro career, Mr. Gurley.

Chapter 33: K. Michelle

K. Michelle is a beautiful woman and talented as well. Her security guards are a bit over zealous. As we approach the lower level of the airport for departure no one was around. No cars, no people, unusually slow. The guards jump out of the limo and tell no one to move, like we are a Brinks truck loaded down with gold. One guard is spastically running around, I found it comical. Talk about over doing it. Finally, he opens the door for K. Michelle and her assistant and I assist with the luggage. Before I could turn around they were entering the airport. I return to the driver's seat and I noticed a gift bag in the back seat. How sweet! They didn't tip me but left me a surprise. To be sure, I phone the assistant and tell her of the bag. She says, "Oh thank you so much, that is a gift for a friend." I return to the place I dropped them and she met me and thanked me and asked for my card, as to send a Christmas gift to me. I wonder what Christmas she meant? Oh well, I wish K. Michelle the best.

Chapter 34: The Help

Roc Manoff, I am thinking what an unusual name. To my delight it was Octavia Spencer, one of the best of the best of actresses. Tonight, I am on a charter with Octavia to the premiere of the Red Band Society. Afterwards she came out with a handsome actor from a series called Brothers and Sisters, I cannot recall his name. Octavia was carrying her high heels and wearing slides. She directed me to a beautiful home in Buckhead for an after party. On the way, she opened a gift from a friend that was a mason jar of moonshine. Oh, my I had a shot of moonshine in my younger days and that was the only one. I thought the top of my head was going to blow up. As they exit the limo I explain where I will be parked across the street and to call me five minutes before departure. I hand her my card as well and suggest she take my number, as I will pull up to the house on call. She says thank you and tells me she takes care of those women whom take care of her. An hour or so passes and Octavia rings my bell. I tell her I am pulling up. As she enters the limo she introduces me to another great actress Allison Janney, star on the sitcom Mom, and also the handsome guy from Brothers and Sisters. Octavia asked me to drop them off at their residence and it was my pleasure. I must say they had a good time and Octavia was talking about one of the female guests whom was a bit too friendly with her male companion as she says, "What makes her think that he was not with me?" By the way he is married to a beautiful model out of New York. I wish I could remember his name, I can't find it, well I guess I could if I tried hard enough. Anyway, I get the guests to their destinations and Octavia is telling me about the good-looking boyfriend Allison has and how close they are. As I arrive at her home, she tells me she's going to pick up her new BMW in the morning so she'll be doing a lot of her own driving. She asks me to wait as I open her door. She expresses how much she enjoyed my service and gave me a hundred dollar tip. My kind of client, best wishes ma'am!

Chapter 35: Biggie Smalls Tonya

The Gift Mart is in town at the mart. That is where I met Vanna White. She was a model for Catalina swimwear line and I was a petite model for a t-shirt company. In fact, I was one of the first to show the famous Farah Fawcett t-shirt. As I arrive curbside Biggie Smalls daughter Tonya, and a friend enter the limo and I proceed to the hotel. They jump out as Tonya says, thank you. They did not give me time to get out of the limo, and they were gone. Nice to meet you, I think, that was pretty cool to have the legend Notorious's daughter in my limo for a short time. Short and cool is okay with me.

Chapter 36: Dwight Howard's Family

You never know who is who, you service the client as to trip sheet directions. What a joke. Humans change their minds and redirect me and lead me on wild goose chases and this trip is off the chain misleading. I assume I am picking up the athlete Dwight Howard when actually I am picking up a male relative whom has flown into Atlanta escorting Dwight's children. Two little cuties. I am to take them to his house north of town when this gentleman informs me we are going way south to visit the grandparents. A short time later they enter the limo and I am directed to the girlfriend's house and then stop at a store and then three hours later to Dwight's. At this point I am billing for an hourly charter instead of a pick-up drop off. We arrive to Dwight's absolutely magnificent crib. Three gates and arrived. As I exit the limo and open the trunk the houseman is hugging everyone and then hugs me. I tell him I am the driver but I like hugs and we laughed. Out of the corner of my eye, I see a larger than life man. I say to him "My goodness you are a tall drink of water." He hugs the kids, does not say two words to me nor does anyone else and I pause a minute, give up and exit the gates. Then I am thinking WOW REALLY? Oh wel,l it never ceases to amaze me do they not tip or was my service bad? Then I remember I am the best of the best.

Chapter 37: Vampire Diaries

I have to say I have never cared for vampire tales and such. As a child, after school, Dark Shadows was the show not to miss, but I did not have a thing for it. Then later I skipped choir practice of all things with a choir boy to go to Phipps Plaza to see the Exorcist which gave me nightmares and I was forced to confess to Mom. Michael Malarkey and Chris Binochu, actors from Vampire Diaries series, are gracing my back seat. What a couple of hotties. So hot in fact that Michael asked little ole' me to join them for a little party. I turned around drooling over the backseat gazing at them and told him I had garter belts older than him and says "No worries Mama, we will shake the dust off of them." WOW, WOW, AND AGAIN WOW. Naturally, I decline but I will treasure that hot hug good-bye and believe it or not a tip!

Chapter 38: Pollyanna McIntosh - Walking Dead

As Pollyanna approaches me she introduces herself. By the way love the accent. She expresses how she is still a bit intoxicated, that after the shoot she and some friends decided to have several drinks and she decided to stay over in Nashville to visit the Johnny Cash museum. About that time two fans approach her with a poster of cut out photos of her. A little strange if you ask me although no one asked, she signed the poster and we departed. As I am driving she is talking up a storm of her adventure and then she finally slows down to what seemed to be tired. When we arrive, I open the trunk and she grabs her bag and hugs me and slips me a twenty. Live on Walking Dead!

Chapter 39: Sam Champion ABC Meteorologist

This trip sheet tells me of two arrivals. When I greet Sam Champion I ask if his wife has exited the plane. He replies, "No my husband is at home." "Whoops!", I am thinking. Will I ever learn? I don't say another word until I arrive at the hotel, give the luggage to the valet and I am out of there.

Chapter 40: Rebecca Campbell - ABC Back To Back

This one was a dynamo from what I understand and I witnessed just that. I picked her up as well as a co-worker and about a mile away from the airport she says to me, "Turn around please I have left my laptop on the plane. I sat it down on the seat to help an older lady gather her overhead bag and forgot it. It is brand new and I have to have it. You can drop me off or I will pay you extra." Naturally, I return to the airport and grab an umbrella for her. Ms. Campbell runs in as I tell her I will be right here. I suggest she go to the Delta desk to reenter security to the plane. This isn't something just anyone can do. The policeman tells me I can't park there. I ignored him and asked to watch the limo. I explain whom I'm driving and he obliges. Who else could charm like that? About that time Ms. Campbell is in sight, laptop in hand. Yeah! We are off again to the studio and she tips me a fifty. I'd have loved to have had one of the sport umbrellas her greeters had from ABC but I dare not ask.

Chapter 41: Ricky Smiley

What a character. He puts his assistant in the backseat and rides up front with me. A bit unusual and I don't care. I drop them off at the news station for a short taping and while I am waiting Porsha Williams is walking toward my limo. I roll down my window and say "It is nice to see you again." She says "Oh yes I remember you." and enters the station. Not too long after Ricky enters the limo and asked if I would please stop, he wanted a soda then he asks me if I had any change. About then his assistant hands some money over his seat. As he leaves the store a young fan approaches Ricky for a photo. Ricky tells him to pull his pants up before he talks to him. I loved it. See you later Mr. Smiley.

Chapter 42: Dave Chappelle

One in a million. As I enter the venue, it is an old church in downtown Atlanta. Now it is where talent comes to entertain. It is referred to as The Tabernacle, a place where if the walls could talk I would listen. I am to assist with the entourage for none other than Dave Chappelle, comic of all. I am standing three steps down from Dave next to the recording and video guys when Dave is talking about oral sex play by play and I blurt "Does he know this was a church?" About that time one of the guys says "Cynthia you are going to have to be quiet", so I step out. After the show Dave is cool and takes photos and offers up hundred-dollar bills to several fans as well as myself. He shakes my hand and tells me thank you. No, thank you Dave!

Chapter 43: Bare As You Dare Party At Buckhead

Cool another night off, girls dressed in black. We are in a friend's stretch limo that owns Scalini's, a wonderful Italian restaurant. The party is in an old house turned club that is full of character. As I exit the limo with my girls I see Scott Steiner, a WWE wrestler whom had stood me up previously. He had a cast on his arm and I ask if he was okay and if he knew whom I was he replied that he did not so I refreshed his memory. I was looking great if I do say so myself. He says "Oh my that was you?" Oh well, snooze you lose, tee hee hee! Later after the party, my intoxicated friend let go of the driver for reasons I do not know and he drove the limo. Needless to say, we got pulled over. As they handcuff our friend the police allow us to go home. Oh, what a night.

Chapter 44: The Gospel Of Kevin

This handsome, cool classy man reminds me why I love my career. Goodness gracious. In fact, he is so handsome, for the first time ever I went a mile the opposite direction. When I collected myself, brain storming my explanation, I came right out with it." I am exiting to head north, I am embarrassed to tell you I could not take my eyes off of your handsome face." He replies "How could I possibly get mad at that?" Sweet as well, this guy. I tell you if I was younger........ I am back on the planet now and the conversation was delightful. He also accepts my compliment by telling me he had been up working and traveling and certainly was not fresh. Who cares? You are an amazing specimen. He takes his hat off and rubs his head. I made him comfortable. Service. Me behind the wheel, missed exit or not, I am a driver of drivers. I am watching every car, person, animal, stop sign, caution at green lights...you never know unless you watch. Watch the front tires, they will direct, and always if the turn signal is blinking, it works, it does not mean they are turning. We arrive at the new film studio, which used to be a beer plant. Two pretty cast members greet my client. He is in good hands now. I tell him good day. No tip and I do not blame him. I would not nor could not have accepted one. GIDDY-UP.

Chapter 45: Steve Harvey

I have had the pleasure of driving two of the sweetest people, the one and only Steve Harvey's in-laws. An ice storm hit Atlanta during their visit for their daughter's birthday. I was assigned to arrive at the home of Mr. Harvey and escort them to the airport to go home. The power was uncertain and it took a few minutes to get the gate open. I sensed they were a bit nervous to get out on the road so I kept it at a slow speed. Slow is being nice about it. The roads were passable but for their nerves I drove under the speed limit in the right lane. This seemed to take the stress off of all of us. As we are chatting they were telling me of the Rolls Royce Steve bought for their daughter's birthday. I asked if he had the pleasure of driving the Rolls and he said no, he loved his Hyundai. Cute I thought! We arrived safely and said our good-byes. A short time later I had Steve's assistant, nice lady, and last but not least I am excited to get a late-night trip call to arrive for Mr. Harvey himself. The pick-up turned out to be quite unusual. The house man greeted me after security allowed entrance. The house man greets me and I tell him it is good to see him and ask if Mr. Harvey was ready and he asked me to wait a minute and he returns with a pair of Mr. Harvey's pants in a dry-cleaning bag. I was stunned yet remained professional. He tells me their destination is a hotel in Buckhead, wait, and then the destination is International Airport. Off I go with Steve's pants to the hotel. In all my years, this is a usual first. Naturally, I do not ask the pants if they care for a bottle of water, music, news, or if the temperature is comfortable. In reality, the pants may be one of my most quiet, easy clients. I arrive to the hotel and take the pants into the front desk. I return to my limo and anticipate nothing. A few hours later a young couple exits the hotel asking the doorman to direct them to the Harvey limo. He waves to me and I pull up and introduce myself and ask for their names and they tell me. I question if they are the only ones I am taking to International. They tell me, yes, it is just the two of them. The doorman puts their luggage in the trunk. They did not speak a word and both of them stared out their own window.

As I pull up to the curb and exit the limo to gather their luggage they tell me good-bye. One of the most unusual assignments but whatever. Have a nice flight!

Chapter 46: Peter Abitante NFL Commission

An exciting time for me. I am a true football fan and naturally my team is the Atlanta Falcons. Win or lose I stay true to my home town team. The draft is taking place at the Ritz Carlton and the media is everywhere. I am in hopes of getting a glimpse at the players. I cruise the inside of the hotel like a kid in a candy store. To no avail, no eye to eye contact with a professional athlete. I rest for a bit and read until I am called on duty. The foyer was suddenly slammed with the top dogs, so to speak, of the business. My client and his associates are in anticipation of their limo. I exit my limo and give the name of my client and immediately am approached by Mr. Abitante. He is eager to go, busy you know, and gathers the crew for the jet at the FBO, Fixed Base Operation. A majority of the elite choose the privacy of the Fixed Base Operation. The Ritz offered clients gift coolers with refreshments. As they exited the limo, by the way no luggage, one of the gentlemen offered his cooler as well as his NFL draft lanyard. Oh Boy!!!!! Mr. Abitante thanks me as well as everyone as they exit the limo. Mr. Abitante, took care of me as far as a gratuity goes. As he is shaking my hand he has a folded fifty-dollar bill in his hand. Once again, a class act. You cannot help but be pleased. Good flight guys. Come back again.

Chapter 47: Land Baron - Art Falcone

The meaning of hurry up for nothing takes a whole new meaning. I am assigned to take as directed by charter for one of what I am told by dispatch to be one of the wealthy of the wealthy with nothing but class. So far, I have no idea, only due to not being in his presence. Never set an eye on him in order to serve him. In a perfection mode for the charter there was an accident to work around, and if anyone knows how, it is I. My office called as I am working. I do not talk on the phone especially when I get there and early mode none the less. I answered as I hear with not so much as hello. The voice says to me "I received a call from a co-worker whom said you sped by him like he was sitting still." I replied I am in a hurry and give me the name of that rat. With a heavy breath the reply was "Slow down and be careful, let me know when you arrive." That was nice, they actually cared for a moment. I arrive at the FBO, go in and give the tech the tail number. I love FBO's. Thank goodness this was an hourly and I realized after eight hours either I had been forgotten about or forgotten about. No sight of anyone in my client list and not even a thank you. In reality I was doing my job and I am fortunate to be working. One last thought. Not if but when from hard work and perseverance I acquire very comfortable wealth I am humble as well thoughtful of others. Give back in other words. I am just saying! Later I am trying to grab a trip driving Keith Urban, and then I was switched and missed Lawrence Fishburne. Oh, what a day.

Chapter 48: Bang-Bang NRA Is In Hotlanta!!!!!

The secret service is doing a briefing for the NRA. I am called in by my general manager to discuss the NRA, President Trump, his son Donald Trump Jr., the entire police force it seems and then some surrounding the city. My client appointed is none other than one of the most interesting calm men I have ever spent time with. I fell in awe of none other than Mr. Frank Brownell. What a quiet lady magnet. He requested a female or should I say his secretary, lining up the complete itinerary for the week of the NRA convention. What a privilege as well as an honor to be selected and respected to complete my assignment beyond the call of duty. My first meeting with Frank as he directed me with a smile. He said his father was Mr. Brownell and please call him Frank. Yes of course. Frank is accompanied by an assistant and he is a font of information. Cool dude and knowledge like none other when it comes to guns. Inside and out. Must admit I was getting the fever. I have been in fear of my life a time or two. I do not know if I have what it takes to pull the trigger. It is late in the day and the schedule does not get heavy until the next morning. I am at the elevator door with a smile at attention. I lead Frank and Dave to the limo to drive to the convention center hotel for full day. A tour of for a few hours at the center and off to dinner at the Porsche distribution office. Pretty cool. It was a dinner for Gold Jacket. I asked a lot of questions and found out that you had to donate at least a million. I asked Frank why he was not wearing his jacket and he replied that he kept it in his closet to refrain from being a braggart. That's what his father would have done. Adorning their gold NRA members enjoyed great food and conversation. Back to the hotel. Early next morning a breakfast at the Ritz and then lunch and cocktails at Southern followed by a party later at the Fox Theatre where Donald Trump Jr. is making an appearance, then back to the hotel. Early morning, I greet Frank and Dave and President Trump is coming in town today for a rally. As I open Frank's door and he stands in front of me I am comfortable at this point to straighten his collar. As I do I see a neon art form on his neckline. When I inquire Dave blurts as Frank walks ahead "The art is tropical neon fish all over Frank's body" and I say "All over?" And Dave says "Yes all over" and again I say "All over?" Dave replies "yes all over" and I say ouch and then he tells me he has the name of his proctologist across his bum. HELL O RUSS. Wow, talking about going out with a BANG!!!!!! The secret service is apparently expecting protesters at the rally today with the President coming in town. Security is naturally heightened and the media is in place. The Presidential convoy takes the President to the underground entrance to the Congress Center. Security is so tight I am only allowed to watch via monitor in a room next to the rally. It was still cool. The next day they are inducting Frank's son, as the chairman of the board. Bittersweet day today. It is the day of Frank's departure and the last day the NRA is in town. I took the opportunity, to visit as many booths as I could. My favorite, was the Shoot Like A Girl booth. I bought a couple of t-shirts. I often wonder how Frank and Dave are doing. Give them a call. Frank was a generous tipper. And hugged me good-bye. It was all my

pleasure Frank.

Chapter 49: Going Out With A Real Bang

I am assigned to a week of driving the cast of Growing Up Hip-Hop: Ayanna Fite, Beastie Boys, DJ Hurricane's daughter. I am taking her to the local news stations and radio as well for interviews for the new reality show Growing Up Hip-Hop. Lil' Wayne's daughter Bow Wow, Waka Flocka, etc. The next couple of days are spent getting ready for the premiere at the Woodruff Arts Center. Everyone was dressed to the hilt and dignified. We exit the Art Center, and by the way Ayanna was with a few friends and they are having a good time. We reach the after-premiere party at Club Opium, which by the way is the same club I was standing at when shots were fired, so I am a bit unnerved during the BET awards. This event has all the cast and several of their family members and close friends attending. I pull to the curb and ask Ayanna to contact me fifteen minutes before departure. The party is set to end at midnight. It starts raining and guests are starting to leave. I am standing outside my limo with an umbrella anticipating my clients' exit. The greeter for the event asks me to pull my car up to the entrance to keep my clients dry. As I pull to the curb my client's mother and grandmother are exiting, shots were being fired. At whom and from where I do not know I am not going to stick around and find out. I tell the greeter to put as many people as she can in my limo, everyone is in a panic and I speed off to safety. In the meantime, Ayanna's mother is screaming "If any of my family gets hurt I will sue We TV!" I turn to her and tell her to duck and is that what she is thinking right now, WOW! People never cease to amaze me. How they went from classy to hood behavior in a matter of a few blocks is crazy. I have to say I am pretty sure I do not look good with blood stains and I am not trying to find out. I never heard what happened after I left with my clients to get them home and they were so intoxicated they were happy to be breathing in and out. I explained to my manager I did not want to do anymore hip-hop or rap clients anymore, not ever again but for some reason the request for a female driver with seniority keep coming in and I am the only one to fill the position.

Chapter 50: Lil' Wayne - Last But Not Least

A name I have heard for a long time and never dreamed I would be in the presence of. An unusual amazing human such as Lil' Wayne. His daughter is graduating from high school and three of us have been chosen to get the crew to and from. It starts with an early arrival on Friday morning the day of the graduation ceremony at the private FBO. Of course, they are two hours behind and when the crew opens the door to the jet a cloud of smoke billows before we see the gang. As they come down the stairs Lil' Wayne appears and I could not believe my eyes. He is little. The woman accompanying him looks to be of a Latino heritage and not a smile. The rest of the crew were as awesome and friendly as I could hope. We put everyone and all the luggage in the limos and we are off. It is always cool to watch passersby try to figure out what and whom are in the limos. We arrive at the hotel and we are to be at the World Congress Center at an appropriate time before the ceremony to get Lil' Wayne in his seat in a quiet manner as to keep the focus on the graduates.

That is what this is all about, not the fact that one of the legends of rap is in the house. I am getting a bit nervous because time is getting close and no one is in sight to depart. We inform the bodyguard it is time to leave and he tells us they are getting ice for Lil' Wayne. Ice, I blurt! We have ice and have been told that if we are not there at the appointed time security does not care who we are they will not let us in. Come to find out it is the school police in charge and they do not budge on the rules. That being said finally we are off to the event and just in time. We pull into the lower garage back entrance of the Congress Center and the gang enters the ceremony. All went well with keeping a low profile and afterwards his daughter and a few friends enjoyed a cap and gown photo with Lil' Wayne. Off again back to the hotel. We are to attend a graduation party at the home of Jarrett Jack NBA player. What a mansion if I do say so. The party was for family and friends and was a pool party that appeared from where I was standing to be reserved. Shortly the gang enters the limos and we are off to the hotel again. Everyone is constantly rolling blunts and getting stoned. No wonder they go back to the hotel. I would have to lay down as well if I smoked that much. Time goes by and the other drivers and I decide to get a menu from Del Frisco's in Buckhead. It is in the parking lot behind the Mandarin Oriental Hotel. As we are eating one of the other drivers says to me "Look Cynthia, know who those women are?" I blurt out that they look like call girls and the bodyguard is greeting them. Who do you think you are talking to? I knew then it was going to be a long wait. To my surprise those particular women came out sooner than expected. My drivers / bodyguards decided to take a siesta. I myself cannot. I have to be aware of what is going on around me at all times. I took photos of both of them asleep with mouths wide open and share the shots with the awakening. I had to have a little fun. Night is upon us now and Lil' Wayne is to make an appearance at one of the local music clubs. Naturally, it seems once again for them to get it together. I am told that it is because of some type of syrup concoction Lil' Wayne drinks. After a few more questions I find out this popular syrup causes convulsions. Really it seems to me I would have to eliminate that from my diet. As we enter the club we are directed to back in by the side entrance and I am bucking. I do not do traps so the other two limos backed in and that left me out front for a quick departure if need be. I am talking with one of the drivers and he says to me "Are my eyes playing tricks on me or is that woman really urinating while texting over there?" "Yes," I reply, "your eyes are on target." About that time, she falls head first onto a sofa sitting outside with her feet in the air and no panties oh my. Lil' Wayne exits the venue in a hurry and I get the creeps. It is never a good sign. Everyone starts piling into the limos and even a few extra bodies. We drive to the Mandarin and shortly after Lil' Wayne comes back to the limo and we are taking he and a couple of the guys to another hotel. As they exit the limo one of the guys tells us they will only need one limo for the duration of the evening and that driver needs to go to the store to get condoms. I look at the two guys whom work with me and tell them to toss a coin. I am exiting the hotel, laughing mostly because NO TIP, when I hear someone yelling my name. I stop and one of the gang asks me if I was straight. I reply, "Yes, what do you mean, I would never come out and ask for a tip." and he invites me to come up to the suite and party naked. BANG BANG GOODNIGHT. GIDDY-UP TIC-TOC.

Lesson 1

Always taking the most resistant path and having to out-do any competition from swim team to camp athletics to boyfriend and friends. I guess it was a demand for attention. Some might call that insane. I considered it a way of life.

Lesson 2

Before I could drive I would work being out there instead of the comfort of my childhood nest. I became street-savvy. These skills were not easily obtained. I have always had an over-the-top reach out and talk to anyone personality (swimming up stream).

Lesson 3

Predators come in all shapes and sizes. Learning to remain calm and safe in most cases was and still is true for me today. "Only by the grace of God." Growing up in big city and working out in public I started at early age.

Lesson 4

Through the years driving some of the biggest and baddest in the hip-hop, rock and roll, professional athletes, and captains of industry, the challenges were sometimes appalling and intolerable. You stick it out and outsmart them.

Lesson 5

I prefer to speak face-to-face with young women on the subject of inner strength. Experience is the best teacher as well as someone like myself who has been in frightening self-preservation circumstances. Whether in social or career situations, how to handle anything.

Again: Only by the grace of God.

Special thanks to Derek, could not have completed it without you my friend and special thanks to Don as well! God bless!

The author Cynthia Kaye is a professional female chauffeur. She is the mother of three beautiful children and is from Atlanta, Georgia.